woodvale

Rachel Madeline

For Kristin
I would be lost without you.

1989

"I've told you my stories for years now. Some have been about coming of age. Some have been about coming undone. This is a story about coming into your own, and as a result... coming alive."

<u>Welcome To New York</u>

Heartbeats riding the late night 1
from Lincoln Center to 103rd,
taxis oozing of drunken laughter
mixed with draining bank accounts,
bustling shoes scraping the pavement
in a rush to reach the big break,
every language known by humanity
mingling together in darkened alleys.
It's the voice of a city that doesn't sleep
coaxing me to rest my weary head
and welcoming me home.

<u>Blank Space</u>

You can call me everything
they say I am
sadistic
vindictive
lecherous
reckless
insane
as long as you also call me
yours.

Style

Even after the walls crumbled,
for the hundredth time in a row,
my fragmented soul chose you.
Through all the trials and tribulations
I remain an ever-hopeful masochist,
a true resident of Dante's third circle.

<u>Out of the Woods</u>

Why is the sky falling?
Is today the day?
Do we know?
Was that the last straw?
Are we done?
Can you look at me?
Is it over?
Do we walk away?
Why do my eyes burn?
Are you crying too?
Is my chest supposed to hurt?
That's it?

<u>All You Had to Do Was Stay</u>

I painted you on card stock
floods of images
in black
the color of permanence.

When it started to rain
I prayed for the pages
to bleed
a river of ink down the storm drain.

<u>Shake It Off</u>

All those silly little names
you call me in private
and those silly little rumors
you whisper in bathroom stalls
and those silly little looks
you toss me in the street
and those silly little things
make for excellent music;
the beat of my own existence
skipping down Broadway
inconveniencing your every day.

I Wish You Would

picking petals off white roses
watching them fall to the ground
a carpet of scented snow

in a plush, pillowy field
searching low and high in the grass
for a four-leaf nestled among three

the softest plunk
of the coin held warm in a back pocket
sinking in the water of the deepest well

closed amber eyes
as the night sky cheers loudly
for the stars sprinting to the finish line

imploring and beseeching
for any sign of luck from the Heavens
that wishing for you was enough

Bad Blood

Your name used to be served
for dessert in conversation;
honey freshly poured from the jar
into a glass of sifting leaves
with a splash of cubed sugar.

Now it's served as the salad
a display rich in iron
from the spinach to the blood;
an appetizer of betrayal
to go with your performative sorry.

Wildest Dreams

Looks like you have a stalker
hiding behind a newspaper
across from you at the cafe on 4th St,
humming motown on the fire escape
on the other side of the breakfast nook,
leaving kiss marks of red lipstick
against the bedroom window glass,
knocking on the front door at 3 am
before picking the lock.

You can't call the cops
how could they arrest a phantom
who shares the bedroom eyes
I left you with years ago.

How You Get the Girl

You have to swear
on the Bible
on the steps beneath your feet
on the crying sky
on your mother's future grave
on your father's absence
on your sister's marriage
on your heart
on my mind
that sorry doesn't even begin
to describe what you feel
and that letting me slip away
like water from the Thames
is the greatest tragedy
to befall any love drunk soul.

This Love

Just like that
you've rushed in
smothering my feet in Pacific water
cold to the touch
a dart of shivering salt
kissing at my soles.

And just like that
you pull away once more
recede into the endless murky blue
vast to the eye
massacring my peace of mind
taking part of my spirit.

Please come again soon.

I Know Places

Hunting was our specialty,
for fame and each other,
chasing love hidden in the grass
to take back to base camp,
pitched with tents of notoriety.

Whispers in the newsprint brush
change the game,
the chilling camera clad clarity
we are no longer the hunters
we are now the prey.

<u>Clean</u>

When a tree falls in a dense forest it still makes a sound, whether or not anyone was around to hear it. The branches flail through the air, screaming silently, until the body hits the ground with thunderous applause. Its core shatters into millions of tiny splinters that thicken the air in inadequacy. The ultimate karmic sign of breaking down the old and beginning anew.
Is the same true for drowning? When the water rushes in through the airways and coats the voice box, can anything be heard? Will the screams just form speechless bubbles that rise to the surface? And when all hope is gone, that someone will come to the rescue, is that the moment when all meditated sins wash away into the void? Is that when the weight of lost love and night gripped pain leaves the hollowed-out home of ligaments and diffuses with the salt?

Is that when I can finally stop holding my breath? Is that when I will feel alive again?

Will I float?

<u>Wonderland</u>

When I eventually go mad
stuck in this misdirected maze
we've fallen into
filled with garden song and disdain
for our reckless, weed sprouted souls
over the clink of tea being poured
to wandering, devilish eyes
that scream "turn back",

will you demand my head
on a silver spoon platter
or let me continue
painting your topiaries
the shade I bleed for you?

<u>You Are In Love</u>

8 p.m.
a Tuesday
in January
my thumbs lightly tapping the illuminated keys
no hesitation
no second guessing
the letters string together a phrase
a funny combination of vowels and consonants
reading it over before pressing send
now there is hesitation
now there is second guessing
rationalizing over and over
it's too early to be true
we barely know each other
there's just no way

the minute I tried to put you down
deny what I had said
was the moment I knew it was true

New Romantics

There's so many things I want:

to risk freezing stumbling home at 4 a.m.
drinks with the band after a show in Berkeley
a mascara downpour in the bathroom of a hotel bar
clothes that would make my grandmother pray for me
my name permanently sucked on by some middle-class gossip
leaving my heart stranded at the Market Street station.

Am I damaged enough to have that all for free?

reputation

"Let me say it again, louder for those in the back . . . we think we know someone, but the truth is that we only know the version of them that they have chosen to show us. There will be no further explanation. There will just be reputation."

. . . Ready For It?

Are you afraid?
Should I be?
Should I heed your warnings?
Should I turn and run like
a child from the monsters under the bed?
Should I cut my losses now
settling for a what might have been
instead of what we can become?
Should I write you a letter
thanking you for the last few months
and coldly leave it on your pillow
so your face won't change my mind?

Why should I be?

End Game

The very first time
your hands laid against my skin
you bled
slowly seeping through the epidermis
past the veins
conversing with the circulating blood
down into the pits
past all the bones and the organs
until striking gold
on my snow tainted soul.
You trickled
until the stark void of color
smiled back
gleaming in opalescence.

I Did Something Bad

Who could've predicted
the strongest form of currency,
above the dollar and the pound,
would be a sentence rolling
off your venomous forked tongue
with my name at the end of it?

Don't Blame Me

My thoughts run rampant
a stampede in a gorge,
wild and domineering.
My actions tell stories
strawberries dipped in sin
served over pots of tea to good wives.
My name is whispered
weaving in between the pews
tasted by the whole congregation.
My reputation precedes me
just another godforsaken addict,
constantly high on blue eyes.

<u>Delicate</u>

You're what I crave.
A beacon of love
or a guise of hope.
Whimsically soft
and iridescently beautiful.
The Heavens bestow you to me
falling gently in the air.
But one moment you're here,
in next you're gone
just in a puddle in my hand.

Can I catch you again?

<u>Look What You Made Me Do</u>

How does it feel
to see the face of a girl
you prematurely pronounced dead?
Is it the eyes full of life that haunt you?
Or the maybe the nose
freckled with the soil of petty lies
you poured on top of an unmarked grave?
Perhaps it's the cherry red lips
curled into a fresh picked smile
stained with day old blood.

You prayed for demise and karma,
believing the divine view you
as a self-proclaimed saint
but God does have favorites
after all.

So It Goes

Shuffle once
twice
three times.
Let the jumpers fall where they may.
The king of cups.
The queen of swords.
Fold them over more
and more until the magic
presses pause on the mixing.
Lay them out,
methodically with intent;
Guide your hands
to the source of the energy,
your destiny awaits.

The lovers.

<u>Gorgeous</u>

My hatred for your laugh
chisels Michelangelo dimples
into my rose bitten cheeks.
Your cloudless summer day eyes
paint me a new shade of green
as I imagine the manicured hands
that run through your hair
at 2 a.m. on a Wednesday.
That demeanor, casual and cool,
coddles my dreams -
a dangling carrot of
what I can't have.

I would set every city ablaze,
let the ashes fall over the
cynical and broken hearted
just to take you home
to me.

<u>Getaway Car</u>

Soft snores escape chapped lips
under a polyester duvet
that shouldn't see black light.
Neon signs and empty promises
hover in the stale air
of a room broadcasted as vacant
until five hours ago.
They settle in the indentation,
my shoulders left on the mattress
that was purchased in 1989
it has never been replaced,
still seeping with adrenaline filled regret.

The engine coming to life
as I shove the keys in the ignition
followed the crunch of tires
pulling off the gravel
and onto the cold asphalt
is the only form of
goodbye and closure
I can offer you.

King Of My Heart

I used to trace my scars at night,
the faint and the deep,
little reminders of my inadequacy.
I could have drawn a map from memory,
a trail around town of the failures
endured in passenger seats
or over wine at the chef's table.

Under the gaze of your smile
and the warmth of the sweater
you gifted me from your closet,
the cracks turn into sugar dust
sweet crystalline
suited just to your taste.

Was I ever in love before you?

Dancing With Our Hands Tied

When the sky falls
and the earth crumbles like fresh pastry
and there's nowhere left to take cover
and the air is equal parts scream and oxygen
and the world as we know it is lost to a sea of terror
I hope you still hear the music
and dance with me again.

Dress

Quaking hands hold glasses of champagne.
Blood racing at every minuscule brush.
Eyes frantically search for a private oasis.
Heart pounding to metronome footsteps.
Cool lips against flushed neckline skin.
Labels previously assigned dissolve against heated breath.

Each syllable of my name
pulls the zipper down further
until I'm wearing only you.

This Is Why We Can't Have Nice Things

It's a good thing I kept an atlas
directing me to the hatchet we buried
beneath the elephant shaped topiaries
adjacent to the lawn facing East Egg.
Dirt warms itself beneath my nails,
convening to the sound of sheet steel
intently breaking the soil
until connection with a handle
forged from the tallest oak
in the forest of false empathy.

Alert the authorities,
there's a mad woman on the loose
with apathetic eyes and a malefic smile.

She is not offering last words.

Call It What You Want

I built this house on my own,
filled every room with trinkets
shaped like all my successes
to curb the taste of loneliness.
The storm rung these walls dry,
weathering the exterior to bones,
devaluing all possessions within
including me and my empty triumphs.
These halls welcomed in frost,
froze me into a glacier of shame
until one day you built a fire
thawed the past away drip by drip
until I sat in a puddle on the floorboards
brand new.

New Year's Day

My soul melts in your hands:
dripping through the crevices between the fingers
onto the hardwood imprinted with our dance steps;
a coruscating pool of forgotten child dreams
stirred with journal logged heartache.

We can scrub these floors together
just you and me
and my spirit
reimagined from your eyes.

Lover

"I've decided that in this life, I want to be defined by the things I love- not the things I hate, the things I'm afraid of, or the things that haunt me in the middle of the night. Those things may be struggles, but they're not my identity. I wish the same for you."

<u>I Forgot That You Existed</u>

Keys that were just in my hands,
hair elastics that never come home,
glasses I last saw in my car,
the tv remote collecting dust somewhere,
the idea of your existence.

All memorabilia washed up on the shore
of the forgotten and the damned.

Cruel Summer

Start small.
Keep it reasonable.
A night in the hotel off Park
complete with turn-down service bright and early.
I'll call.
Advance you one better.
The key under the pot out front
left there for your midnight house call.
You think I'm bluffing.
Add more to the pile.
One lime green toothbrush on the counter
freshly purchased, still in the box.
Time to raise the stakes.
Bet more than I bargained for.
Allusions to you in all of my writing
a figment of what I want most.

Show your hand
complete with your ace
I'll show you mine
a full house of hearts.

<u>Lover</u>

joint signatures
matching bath towels
color coordinated outfits
adjoining chairs
combined income
dual closets
shared promises

all things sorted and paired
forever

The Man

9
you're worrying too much
if a boy is mean they like you
but don't be mean back
that's not very ladylike
12
the hem must be fingertip length
too much skin is against the dress code
your shoulder could prove too tempting
for your male classmates
16
no one is going to listen to you
if you're too aggressive with your opinions
a nice girl
doesn't say the word "fuck"
20
these office hours are for engineers
the plaid skirt and big brown eyes
tell me you're in the wrong place
the English department is across campus
25
stop being so sensitive
don't take yourself so seriously
you're just another stuck up bitch
with a college degree

The Archer

sweat pooling in the indentations of my forehead
the thermal sheets creasing under my clammy grip
each breath sprints after the last one
hands above my head, holding the nape of my neck
until my lungs find air-conditioned equilibrium
you stir gently
rolling over onto your left side to face me
everything ok?
mumbled in a freshly woken drawl
corneas flick towards the cream entryway
there's no sign of it
I swear I just saw it
you blanket my right hand with your still palm
softening my fistful of bed linen
nothing, just a silly dream
I can make out the outline of your smile
as you drift back to sugarplum slumber
my mind stays glued to the door
did you stash your go bag before my eyes noticed?
is it hiding beneath the bed as we speak?
am I just hallucinating?
your lofty snore shakes me out of mania
I watch your chest move slowly a moment more
please don't leave me

I Think He Knows

Licked scarlet lips
pulling a tied cherry stem
from between their divide.
Freshly painted golden nails
the correct length to mark a back
tap impatiently against the table.
Eyes that glow in the overhead lighting
slowly but carefully undoing each button
unwrapping a silk adorned gift.

Let's stop pretending
that your answer will be no.

Miss Americana & the Heartbreak Prince

You created America's sweetheart
a star-spangled glittery porcelain doll,
displayed her in the National Gallery
next to George Healy's oil on canvas,
indoctrinated her to be a polite girl
with her neatly tied, bow bound dresses,
claimed her as your own in red ink
a shiny example of Americana.

Is that why it hurt so deeply
when fate whispered to her
to not go silently?

Paper Rings

Turn it once
watch the quarter disappear.
Turn it twice
hear the gears crunchy grind.
Turn it three times
spokes aligning to their spots.
Out pops the container,
clear, cheap plastic
with a violently pink lid
hoarding beloved treasure -
spray painted gold
twisted into a circle
holding a specious gem.
The perfect paradox
for our love.

<u>Cornelia Street</u>

The floorboards groaning
as you hummed cool jazz
against the quartz counter
with city morning light
grazing a baby blue icebox.

In that homespun moment
I abandoned my practice
left my altar behind on scraps
of half-written, drunken lyrics
and prayed to you, my miracle.

Death By A Thousand Cuts

The worst pain of all
wasn't the yearning at 1 a.m.
for the shape of another
to drape their arms around me,

or trying to scrub the memories
of touch on my hips, heart, and soul
until the skin laid raw with regret,

it was my heart murmuring
you deserve better
while my head cut to the bone.
This is all you deserve.

London Boy

Of Light,
of Hundred Spires,
of Brotherly Love,
of Lilies,
of the Sun,
the Magic,
the Emerald,
the White,
the Mile High,
the Eternal.

I gift them all time
but leave my heart
in a flat in Town.

<u>Soon You'll Get Better</u>

How am I supposed to be strong
for the strongest person I know?

False God

Confess to me.
In that hushed voice, mutter your sins while
the air fills with the sound that fall from my lips
as you discover places on my sacred body
no other soul has dared to venture before.
Praise me.
Speak only breathy flatteries of the sweetness
dripping off my skin and the endless ecstasy
radiating through every inch of my flesh.
Worship me.
Pour your eyes into mine,
clasp the curve of my hips,
drink the cocktail of our sweat
and pray that I lead you to Paradise.

I am the judge and jury, your only Savior.
Show me you deserve salvation.

You Need to Calm Down

If you are satisfied with your service
be sure to visit our website
and fill out a quick survey.
If you would like to file a complaint
instead of acting like a decent individual
who believes in equal opportunity and rights
please hang up and never call again.

Afterglow

When the lights turn off,
in the faint traces that occupy the air
Aphrodite buries a golden casket
filled in its entirety with ashes;
shared domesticated dreams
jointly paid leases
drunken I love you's
intimately known jokes
take their final resting place.
At the foot of the tombstone,
bathed in hues of purple remorse
you will find me there
waiting for your patched up heart
to hand me a shovel and start digging.

<u>Me!</u>

Dull conversation takes a seat at the table,
swirls its index finger around in the wine
picking lightly at the entree in front of you.
It watches your mouth open cautiously,
giggling as the words get caught in your throat
your lips releasing a disappointed sigh.
This presence is normally unwelcomed
left on the stained mat out front,
but that's only when you sit across from me.

<u>It's Nice To Have A Friend</u>

If you lead me into the dark
I will follow all the way
blindly stumbling around
drenched in first love faith
loyal to the garden of our bond.

__Daylight__

my back against the wall
the blue paint cool to the touch
bloodshot pulsating from the strain
of constant adjusting to broken gloom

your right hand on the pull cord
eyes never leaving my face

pull the shades
flood me with hope again
drown me in daytime sun

I dare you

folklore

"Picking up a pen was my way of escaping into fantasy, history, and memory. I've told these stories to the best of my ability with all the love, wonder, and whimsy they deserve. Now it's up to you to pass them down."

the 1

The greatest loves, the ones studied in classrooms for ages to
come, are documented.
It could be in words: letters with indentations of yearning in the
pages, song lyrics made general for the public with nods of privacy
interwoven, prose submitted to a publisher who may or may not
question if this round is autobiographical or just another
production of a romantic's mind.
It could be visual: photographs taken on disposable film carefully
unexposed to light, paintings done in palettes with the colors of
sun-bleached hair and early morning eyes, architecture mimicking
intimately known curves of hips.

I'd like to believe we were a film.
Every inconsequential moment where you would linger on my lips
just a fraction too long or you changed the radio in your hand-me-
down car to a song I could hum to or our fingers unknowingly
brushing reaching for keys on the kitchen counter. Each second
imprinted on thirty-five millimeter.

Should I press play knowing how it ends?

<u>cardigan</u>

Wisdom comes with age, that's the way the saying goes, right?
With each passing year, the more you learn about the world and
acquire a deeper understanding about the truths that make it turn.
Being young equates to having ill formed opinions and a lack of
knowledge to have a clear perspective on life.

But at eighteen, I knew your gait as you weaved between people
on the sidewalk, the smirk three Jack and Cokes drew on your face,
the sound of your boots walking out the front door and down the
weathered porch steps, the cry of your 3 am phone call reeking of
regret, and your eyes filled to the brim with pleading desperation.

Even in my youth, I knew everything about you.

the last great american dynasty

I've stayed too long
with the rusted joints
creaking at each subtle breeze
the salt air blesses the coastline with.
I am weathered
from gaudy, champagne parties
filled with notable figures
and stolen moments of privacy
worthy of newspaper headlines.
I stand tall
waiting, yearning for restoration
at the hands of a wandering soul
scarred and drenched in blue ink
fiending for something new.

exile

people see what they want to see
optimism while standing over decay
kindness in place of wanton cruelty
a bliss filled morning while mourning
love -
love in moments steaming in regret

maybe that's why you only remember my eyes
when my feet were already out the door

<u>My Tears Ricochet</u>

It's been years since you thought of me.
denial
The memory of me in the back of your closet
anger
tucked away amongst the Christmas gifts you have no use for.
bargaining
Always just a few steps away
depression
from unearthing my gift of grief.
acceptance

Which stage were you in
when they lowered my body into the ground?

mirrorball

it's all a balancing act

one arm's length forward
showing unspoken dreams
a bend backwards
mirroring the past
a stabilized core holding center
gleaming in present day

hovering above in the air
the star sign of early June
just a breeze's touch
from meeting a less interesting
fate

seven

the solutions seemed so simple
when the universe began at my bed,
the seams of the floral comforter
turned up to protect me from falling over
edges of the known world drawn in crayon,

and ended at the edge of town,
where we'd walk to with our backpacks
filled with toys and an extra sweater
as we'd wait for wind to blow us over
and into undrawn corners of an expanding map

<u>august</u>

I would choose you
with your sun painted back
and hair spun by the gods
blowing in the salt kissed air.

I would choose you
as your laugh vibrated against
the disheveled cotton sheets
we called our secret home.

I would choose you
while you stand in the garden
equating the heart I gave you
to just a summer thing.

Even with the chronic ache
burying itself in my chest
I would choose you over me
every
single
time.

<u>this is me trying</u>

Sweet soul,

I woke up today and didn't pick myself apart in the bathroom
mirror. I got out of bed before noon and made myself a cup of
coffee so that I could brave the day with caffeine roaring in my
bloodstream. I sat at my kitchen table in silence, my intrusive
thoughts rarely share dinner with me anymore. I visited with
friends and let my face twist and hang in any shape it so desired
without a twinge of guilt to utter "I'm fine". As I drove home, I
took my time around each winding turn, savoring every fleeting
moment of given time I have been blessed with. I know I'll go to
sleep tonight without dreading tomorrow or lingering in a void of
grief-stricken thought.

Every tiny step you take now, every extra breath that rolls from
your lips and into the dry air, every single time you can admit to
yourself that you are not ok matters.

It gets better. You get better. We get better. And I'm proud of you.

<u>illicit affairs</u>

You told me life is colorful
when you're hopelessly in love
and with you I saw them all;
every shade and blend,
a palette crafted from love.
Impressionism in my pupils,
each moment a Monet crafted
just for me.

Now the world sits blank,
an empty canvas,
an evocative void of emptiness
glaring at me in stale white.

invisible string

one moment
flickering in overhead lighting
it's you
the face I imagine onto all of my dates before the entree
the voice in the back of my head telling me I could do better
the phantom in my dreams caressing my cheeks
the eyes that can drag me into an early grave
one moment
bathed in ruby red
gone is the life I had before you

mad woman

behind every strong woman
is a slanderous mob
mouths foaming with bloodlust
teeth sharpened and bared
waiting to go for the throat
craving the sight of putting a rabid animal
down for good

epiphany

preparation, that's the most we can do
prepare and prepare and prepare
read textbooks stuffed with the words of the older and wiser
take courses that mimic hands-on experience
beat our knuckles bloody, squeeze out every drop of sweat
until deemed ready in flying colors

but it's not enough until
you're willing to give your last breath
and every ounce of your soul
to a cause that may be all but lost

betty

Stop. Please just fucking stop. I don't know what you expected by
coming here today. What exactly do you want me to do? Forgive
you? Just like that? Like you didn't make me feel like I am less
than nothing? Like the world I have known didn't completely
shatter into bits of insecurity? Like every single demon I have has
taken on the shape of you and whispers to me every single
goddamn day that I have never been good enough? You can blame
your age or my friends who never liked you or that it was just a
lapse in judgment, but that "mistake" was paid for by me not you.
We both lost me, and I'm going to spend a lifetime trying to
recover what died while you live with the regret. I hope it eats you
alive, chews you up, and spits you back out over and over again. I
hope you never feel as happy as you did with me ever again. So
just leave. Don't ever come back. I hope the summer was worth it
because I clearly wasn't.

peace

strike on box
those words feel distant, a lifetime ago
they've blurred under the haze of ash
the walls disintegrating to specks of dust
brought down by flames my match lit
I tell you to go
find solace elsewhere
build a home with someone nice
somewhere where the sun rises every day
and the rain only welcomes in Spring's touch
you take a seat next to me
inhale a wave of obsidian smoke
the blue of your eyes quenches my thirst
I've always hated the cold

<u>hoax</u>

I stopped believing in magic long ago.
All the tricks became easy to debunk
when you knew what to look for -
a bit of plexiglass here,
one or two hidden compartments there.
I stopped believing in magic long ago.
Soft white lies on my pillow,
deceptive words pressing down on scars,
boring arguments over breakfast
became a daily occurrence.
I stopped believing in magic long ago.
But, with you I'll lie
to myself and anyone who cares to ask
that this love still breathes crisp mountain air.
You know I'll never leave.

the lakes

paint me
among the dew kissed grass
adorned with honeysuckle hair
and glacial whirlpool eyes
paint me
fashioned so Calliope may know
the touch of satin clad jealous rage
as the poets site only my name
at the beginning of glorious epics

evermore

"I have no idea what will come next. I have no idea about a lot of things these days and so I've clung to the one thing that keeps me connected to all of you. That thing has and always will be music. And may it continue, evermore."

<u>willow</u>

fool me once
shame on you
fool me twice
take the lead
I'm coming with you

<u>champagne problems</u>

To you, our love was always Cristal:
so rare people die yearning for one taste.
The chosen drink of aristocrats and royals,
all yours to be drunk off of for free.

To me, we tasted exactly the same as
a bottle from the market around the corner:
comforting and satisfactory in every way
with a price tag to match the mediocrity.

I was so intoxicated by our adequacy
it took you to bend down on one knee
for my inebriated soul to reach sober clarity,
telling you three words I always knew.

I'm so sorry.

<u>gold rush</u>

a dreamers hands
knee deep in the Sacramento
following a pipedream
golden strands to match
a set of uneven opals
dirt in my nail beds
panning away reality
you're there
I know you are
let me strike upon you

'tis the damn season

Softened flannel sheet heaven.
Bird sung melodies in the air.
The shape of your bare chest
molded against my shoulder blades.
Familiarity pulls your lips open
blessing the air with my name.

On Monday, the door will close
with smell of my hair in the pillowcases
as the only proof I was ever there.
Those fleeting moments where I thought
maybe those eyes would beg me to stay
tricked me harder than April Fools' Day.

<u>tolerate it</u>

The temple erected bearing your name
has my fingerprints on every stone,
my adoration mixed with the mortar.
Stained glass that matches your eyes
paints the pews as dawn pours through
warming the glacial, unmoving air.
In the middle of the floor, front and center,
you'll find me kneeling at your soulless altar
begging and beseeching for a mere sign.

Show me you see all the work I do.
Show it's not just me who cares.
Show that this isn't all in my head.
Show me you love me too.
Show me you love me.
Love me.
Please love me.

no body, no crime

pockets full of smooth stones
the same weight of executed sins
heave the bag up to the edge
one
two
three
cicada's funeral march cut by the splash
flesh not fresh enough to entice gators
sink deeper in the water
clear as his judgment once was

enjoy the afterlife
see you in the outer ring of the seventh soon

happiness

my grip holds on too tightly
I can't let go
I don't want to
because what is there left when I do?
Just a pack of stiffened joints
with muscle memory of a body
I know too intimately to be strangers
but too distant and cold to be friends.
I can't let go
I can't let go
I can't let go
Please don't let me put you down
please don't make me move on
because what is there left when I do?

<u>dorothea</u>

At night in the angel-filled city, sitting alone
periwinkle thoughts drift to a place outgrown:
a town of snow-covered streets once roamed,
a church you once visited to atone,
and a boy who hopelessly stares at the phone
hoping that when you're tired of being known
you'll give him a call and into his arms, rush home.

coney island

Your love bathed me in warmth
lighting up every crevice of the world
painting my skin until I sat there gilded
Apollo's touch rivaling Midas.
The center of the universe
as I knew it to be
with all the planets spinning round
two celestial bound souls.

Off they float, lost
in an endless sea of dust
out of orbit and out of purpose
since our light went dark.

<u>ivy</u>

They say the eyes are windows to the soul.
Through my coffee-stained panes
laid a forest dying in unspoken thoughts
white rot holding on tightly
living, breathing decay destroying dreams.

Every word your lips press to my ears
is a new prayer to Demeter
may she restore the soil of my woodland
bring back the flora and fauna
a breath of fresh life.

cowboy like me

There's something to be said about being afraid.
Being afraid of touch, sex, or even love.
They're not equivalent but nonetheless the same.
If you're afraid of touch, you're afraid of being seen
in a way that makes you tangible
like "I am right here, I am with you".
If you're afraid of sex, you're afraid of being seen
in a way that's more intimate
like "what once was private is now shared between us".
If you're afraid of love, you're afraid of being seen
in a way that's real
like "your soul is enough, you don't need to run from me".

long story short

the anthology of my life
pages and pages
of misdemeanors with temporary happiness
tied to careless names dropped in

the jacket cover mentions my accomplishments
it only describes you

marjorie

the summer has gone
this season of life burns differently
barren, begging white-hot cold
decimating all I've known
faith escapes my weary head
lost
wandering in the storm
the smallest glimpse of life
blue butterfly on my shoulder
puts to bed this winter

welcome home

<u>closure</u>

was this for me
or for your peace of mind?

evermore

not for the faint of heart
or the weak of stomach
all aboard
join me in this expedition
floating along
a sea of dread
home to other souls
lost in the fray
hoist the sails
let the wind push us forward
towards a new dawn we ride
we steer into rogue waves
almost capsizing
chasing death delivered by her majesty
when the clouds break
light grabs hold of the helm
bathes us in her warmth
as we search for signs
along the horizon line
is that it
could it be
hope
bear up
pray for spring tides
hurry now
we need to make port
we need life again

right where you left me

What am I supposed to do?
It's 10 p.m. and a Saturday.
If I stand, I'll tilt over
my bones have reduced to Jell-O
encased in gin-soaked blood.
My head feels like a peach in summer
soft and fuzzy and warm and fuzzy again.
I can't go to the driver's seat
I could hurt someone
worse than I'm hurting myself now.
I should wait here longer.
I'll keep scrolling and scrolling
but the only name that would have cared
belongs to you
and you'll greet me with voicemail.

it's time to go

heal toe heel toe
one foot at a time
let the footsteps ring in the hall
the sound of bravery
going for the door

the only goodbye
that matters

Red – The Vault

"In the land of heartbreak, moments of strength, independence, and devil-may-care rebellion are intricately woven together with grief, paralyzing vulnerability and hopelessness. Imagining your future might always take you on a detour back to the past."

<u>Better Man</u>

There's a tan line around my pinky
on my right hand just below the knuckle.
It has the same opacity as the scars
in the shape of your almond nails
that run the length of my back.
An ever-soft impression on skin
of where red string once laid
tied neatly in a fastidious bow.

My connection to fate
gone and blown away
floating in the breeze.

<u>Nothing New</u>

Are you as bored of me
yet
as everyone else is,
including myself?

Babe

The words sleep soundly
just below the surface
making home in my dermis.
My hands clammy and shaken
try to make them disappear,
rubbing feverishly
so they might evaporate
into my warmed blood
vanishing without a trace.
They attach to my bones
use the marrow as a jungle gym:
swinging against rib cage,
climbing up my sternum
until lodged in my throat;
lightly choking at first
but soon I'm heaving
standing over the bathroom sink
waiting for them to spill
and paint the white marble
a new shade of red.

you promised me
you promised me
YOU promised me
you PROMISED me
you promised ME
you promised me
you promised . . .

<u>Message In A Bottle</u>

Do you need it on paper
spelled out for you
with the letters of the alphabet
in my average handwriting?

Maybe you want to see it
drawn in the daylight
by a pilot whose specialty
is a looping cloud-based script.

Or can you read the stars,
written in blinding light
blinking in fixed position
since the fourth day?

I am yours,
you are mine
just let me know
how you need to hear that.

I Bet You Think About Me

The first rainstorm of the year
where the droplets tap against the window
asking politely to come inside your home
and warm themselves next to the heater.

Vanilla mixed with amber
levitating in the still air of a hotel lobby
dripping in plush crimson velvet
shifting under the gleam of dangling crystal.

Cherry blossoms shedding onto sidewalks,
a blushing springtime snowfall
with fresh tracks on the pavement
resembling size seven boots.

Chipped ironic coffee mugs
decorated in college emblems
or cynical self-deprecating puns
stained at the rim from bags of earl grey.

An apparition of me around every corner,
haunting your every quiet moment
in every seasonal bustling city,
robbing you blind of ever knowing peace.

Forever Winter

Each creak in the floorboards
is another maniacal sea cliff
where the toes of canvas shoes
hover nonchalantly over the edge.
Just one step.
The grandfather clock in the hallway
sings an anthem three times;
it may remain in this family
longer than the pacing, young soul.
Air leaking through cracks in the glass
biting icy viper fangs
envenomating the bloodstream
turning melanin a shade of frost.

Please open the door.
You are not alone.
I am right here.
Please.
Please.
I am begging you.
Please.

Run

The gloss of building lights
reflected in those inkwell pupils
as the Los Angeles skyline passes by
while the headlights carve the I-5
into pieces of night air and pavement.

Baby blue canvas skies
soften against the windshield;
a melting pot of different tones
creating the most striking shade
on God's palette.

Cotton ball fluffed clouds
mimicking the whites of eyes,
that have seen a different sunset
every temperate summer evening,
float through the optimistic sunlight.

I can and will make this highway home,
pitch tents alongside the broken road
uneven with potholes of grieving hearts,
as long as it's his hands on steering wheel
and incandescent smile in the rearview mirror.

The Very First Night

I can still picture it
Westwood
the valet bringing the car around
insisting on the top down
under a pink and orange sky.
Fresh,
young,
and supple.

The beginning of the end.

All Too Well

I was always too something when it came to you:

too loud about my opinions
even though you asked to hear them,
too clingy when I reached for your hand
in front of your condescending friends,
too selfish for asking for a sliver of time
where you could forget the rest of the world,
too emotional for telling you I felt insane
when it was you driving me to the Cliffs,
too young to ever be able to correctly interpret
what you really meant to say during our fights.

In the end,
I was too naive
to believe that I could give you every part of me,

from the innocence I held dear until your smile
convinced me to relinquish it to you
to my eyes that built you cathedrals out of dreams,

and that you had the capacity in your tired soul
to ever love me in the same godforsaken way
I loved you.

ACKNOWLEDGEMENTS

Thank you to Hannah, Cristina, Alie, Kat, Chesney, Kurtie, Johann, Sabrina, Lek, Adria, Anita, and Erin for the support for this book. You all made it possible.

ABOUT THE AUTHOR

Rachel Madeline is a poet from the great state of California. This is her second work of poetry and a continuation of her first book, *swiftly*. She holds a Bachelor of Science in biomedical engineering and is currently an aspiring PhD student of bioengineering. When not in the lab or at work, she can be found wandering around record and bookstores, brewing tea, and dreaming of winter.

Printed in Great Britain
by Amazon

85923211R00062